READY FOR MILITARY ACTION

# MIGHTY
# MILITARY SHIPS

by Marcia Amidon Lusted

**Content Consultant**
Mitchell A. Yockelson
Adjunct Faculty
US Naval Academy

**Core Library**

An Imprint of Abdo Publishing
www.abdopublishing.com

www.abdopublishing.com

Published by Abdo Publishing, a division of ABDO, PO Box 398166, Minneapolis, Minnesota 55439. Copyright © 2015 by Abdo Consulting Group, Inc. International copyrights reserved in all countries. No part of this book may be reproduced in any form without written permission from the publisher. Core Library™ is a trademark and logo of Abdo Publishing.

Printed in the United States of America, North Mankato, Minnesota
092014
012015

Cover Photo: iStockphoto
Interior Photos: iStockphoto, 1; Mass Communication Specialist 1st Class Hendrick Dickson/US Navy, 4; Mass Communication Specialist 1st Class Monique Hilley/US Navy, 6; Morgan Over/US Navy, 9; Mass Communication Specialist 2nd Class Kenneth G. Takada/US Navy, 12; US Coast Guard/AP Images, 14; US Naval History and Heritage Command, 16, 18; Photographer's Mate 1st Class Michael W. Pendergrass/US Navy, 20; Mass Communication Specialist Seaman Alonzo M. Archer/US Navy, 22, 45; Photographer's Mate 2nd Class Johnnie R. Robbins/US Navy, 24 (top); Mass Communication Specialist 1st Class Daniel N. Woods/US Navy, 24 (middle); Photographer's Mate 3rd Class Douglas G. Morrison/US Navy, 24 (bottom); Mass Communication Specialist 1st Class Trevor Welsh/US Navy, 26; Ricky Thompson/US Navy, 28, 31; Shutterstock Images, 32; Mass Communication Specialist 3rd Class Travis DiPerna/US Navy, 33; US Navy, 36; Photographer's Mate Airman Damien Horvath/US Navy, 38; US National Archives/US Coast Guard, 42; Mass Communication Specialist Seaman Apprentice Jesse A. Hyatt/US Navy, 43

Editor: Patrick Donnelly
Series Designer: Becky Daum

**Library of Congress Control Number: 2014944242**

**Cataloging-in-Publication Data**
Lusted, Marcia Amidon.
 Mighty military ships / Marcia Amidon Lusted.
   p. cm. -- (Ready for military action)
ISBN 978-1-62403-653-8 (lib. bdg.)
Includes bibliographical references and index.
1. Warships--United States--Juvenile literature.    I. Title.
623.825--dc23

                                                        2014944242

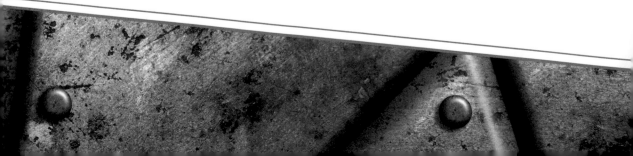

# CONTENTS

# CHAPTER ONE

# TO THE RESCUE

The hull of the USS *Bataan* sliced through the waters off the island country of Haiti. The *Bataan* is an amphibious assault ship built for combat. But on this day the ship had a different mission. Instead of delivering missiles or transporting troops, it was bringing relief supplies.

In January 2010 Haiti suffered a devastating earthquake. The *Bataan* was part of a massive US

Sailors from the USS *Bataan* unload food and water from a landing craft utility vehicle in Haiti to aid in earthquake relief in 2010.

Troops unload heavy equipment from a landing craft unit on the shore of Haiti to help assist with disaster relief in 2010.

military mission that answered the call to help. The ship delivered more than 1,000 pallets of food, bedding, medicine, and other supplies to Haiti. The *Bataan* used its utility boats, helicopters, and special landing craft to move the supplies from the ship to the shore.

A year later, another navy ship was conducting a different kind of mission in the Indian Ocean. The

USS *Carl Vinson* is a nuclear-powered aircraft carrier. It was responsible for transporting the body of terrorist Osama bin Laden after he was killed by US troops in Pakistan. Bin Laden's body was taken aboard the ship and then buried at sea. The US government did not want him to be buried on land. They feared his grave might become a shrine for supporters of terrorism.

In August 2014 the MV *Cape Ray* completed an important mission. It had to neutralize 660 short tons (600 metric tons) of chemical weapons removed from Syria. The specially equipped ship mixed water and other chemicals to deactivate the dangerous weapons. It was the first time that a

## USS *Constitution*

People can still visit one of America's oldest navy ships. The USS *Constitution* is a wooden frigate sailing ship with three masts. It was built in Boston in 1794. The *Constitution* fought in the War of 1812. It has been restored and can still be sailed. It is on display at the Charlestown Navy Yard in Boston, Massachusetts. Visitors can tour the ship. It is the world's oldest commissioned sailing ship that is still afloat.

ship had been used for such a purpose. Because the *Cape Ray* handled the job at sea, it was done quickly and kept the chemicals away from innocent civilians.

## Multipurpose Watercraft

These are examples of how the US Navy's biggest and most amazing ships are used not only for combat and defense but to serve other purposes too. Since its earliest days as a country, the United States has relied on ships for defense, combat, and peacekeeping. Ships helped the United States become a country. Their presence kept other countries from invading

### MV *Cape Ray*

The MV *Cape Ray* started life as a container ship in Saudi Arabia. "MV" stands for "motor vessel." It was used to transport goods. It was purchased by the US Navy in 1993 and put into its Ready Reserve Force. These are ships that can be activated in just five days if necessary. When the navy needed a ship that could be used to neutralize dangerous chemical weapons, the *Cape Ray* was equipped with a special hydrolysis system. This system mixes water and chemicals with the weapon materials to deactivate them.

The *Cape Ray* played a key role in eliminating Syria's chemical weapons materials in 2014.

US waters. They have also gone to the aid of other countries in times of need.

Fulfilling these different roles takes many types of ships. The US military and its partners continue developing new ships to meet the needs of a constantly changing world and to keep up with new technologies. Ships that required thousands of sailors in order to function are being replaced with ships that can be run with much smaller crews. In the future, ships might run on recycled seawater. They could even manufacture their own parts on board.

The *Bataan*, the *Carl Vinson*, and the *Cape Ray* are all prowling the waters of the world. They go where they are needed. They do the jobs they were built to do and many other jobs as well. But to see where these ships came from, it is necessary to start with the earliest days of the navy, when wooden ships patrolled the waters under canvas sails.

## FURTHER EVIDENCE

Chapter One talks about the different roles that US military ships have played over the years. What is the main point of the chapter? What key evidence can you find to support that point? Read the article about the D-day invasion at the website below. Does the information in the article support the main point of the chapter? Write a few sentences using new information from the website as evidence to support this point.

**Library of Congress – D-Day: On the Beach**
www.mycorelibrary.com/ships

Chester Nimitz, a fleet admiral in the US Navy, helped lead his forces to victory in the Pacific Ocean during World War II (1939–1945). He commented on the role of the US Navy in a speech given before his retirement in 1947:

> Defensively, the Navy is still the first line the enemy must hurdle either in the air or on the sea in approaching our coasts across any ocean. The earliest warning of enemy air attack against our vital centers should be provided by naval air, surface and submarine radar pickets deployed in the vast ocean spaces which surround the continent. The safety of our essential trade routes and ocean lines of communication and those of our allies, the protection of areas of vital strategic importance such as the sources of raw material, advanced base locations, etc., are but matters of course if we control the seas. Only naval air-sea power can ensure this. Offensively, it is the function of the Navy to carry the war to the enemy so that it will not be fought on United States soil.

Source: "Employment of Naval Forces." The Navy Department Library. *Naval History and Heritage Command*, n.d. Web. Accessed September 16, 2014.

## What's the Big Idea?

Does this quote still fit the role of today's navy? Should the navy just protect the United States? Or in order to protect US interests, should the navy focus on more than just defense?

# CHAPTER TWO

# THE STORY OF US SHIPS AT SEA

The first US naval ships were frigates, brigs, sloops, and schooners. These were all types of wooden sailing ships with canvas sails. Some were made for fighting. Others were made for traveling quickly.

The United States had a navy nine months before it was actually a country. During the American Revolution (1775–1783), the small US Navy was

A painting depicting the Continental Navy frigate *Confederacy* is displayed at the Navy Art Gallery at the Washington Navy Yard.

US troops unload from a landing barge on the beaches of France during World War II.

outnumbered. The British navy had 270 ships in 1776. The US Navy had just 27. So the United States worked with many privateers. These are ships owned by private citizens. They were hired to fight alongside the US Navy.

US ships interrupted trade by capturing British cargo ships. They kept England from sending more soldiers and supplies to the United States. The British destroyed many of the US Navy's bigger ships. Others were burned by the Americans themselves to keep them from falling into British hands. But with help from France and other allies, the US Navy played a role in winning the war.

After the war, the navy focused mostly on protecting US shores. Eventually, as the country grew stronger, its navy did not wait for trouble to come to it. Naval forces began moving out from home to deal with potential threats.

## The Higgins Boat

One of the most famous boats of World War II is the Higgins boat. These little boats were half wood and half steel. They could land on the beach and had a steel gate that would open to let soldiers get off. Thousands of troops used these efficient landing barges to storm the beaches of France. US General Dwight D. Eisenhower said that the Higgins boats helped win the war because the D-day invasion could not have happened without them.

## Introducing New Ships

As the US Navy began to engage in newer forms of battle, the need for new types of ships continued to grow. Around the time of the American Civil War (1861–1865), wooden ships were covered with iron to protect them from torpedoes and rams. As naval guns

The CSS Virginia—formerly the USS Merrimack—was one of the first ironclads in history.

grew heavier, sturdier ships were necessary to carry them. In the late 1800s the navy began building ships made from iron and steel. These ships were stronger and harder to sink. Submarines also were introduced during the Civil War.

Airplanes became important for the military in the time leading up to World War I (1914–1918). The navy developed aircraft carriers, ships with decks for landing and launching airplanes. The first carrier in 1910 was just a regular ship with a wooden platform built over one end. Eventually carriers would be some of the navy's biggest ships, reaching 20 stories high above the water.

The evolution of military ships continued during World War II. Ships needed to travel farther and carry out roles such as transporting equipment, serving as hospitals, and carrying more soldiers and sailors than ever before. Amphibious ships helped US, British, and Canadian troops land on the beaches of France during the D-day invasion in 1944. These ships could travel on water or land. Special landing craft, which could move through

## Ironclads

The first wooden boats to be protected by iron armor were called ironclads. During the Civil War the Confederate navy from the South was the first to build these ships. One of the most famous examples was the USS *Merrimack*. It had been sunk in the harbor at Norfolk, Virginia. The Confederates salvaged it and rebuilt it as an ironclad. The newly named CSS *Virginia* had iron panels to protect it against cannonballs. It engaged the USS *Monitor* in the Battle of Hampton Roads in 1862. That was the first battle between ironclad ships.

US troops wade ashore from their landing craft during the D-day invasion.

water or onto dry land, were designed to open easily and unload troops quickly.

The navy also built many battleships, battle cruisers, and pocket battleships, which were cruisers with bigger guns. These ships had many different types of guns and armor to protect them. Other ships were built just for launching torpedoes or attacking enemies quickly. The navy needed these new kinds of ships to fight in new ways. Ships no longer just fought other ships. They might have to shoot down aircraft, drop mines on submarines, or fire at targets on land. It took different types of ships to do these things well.

## Army Ships

The US Navy isn't the only branch of the military with its own ships. The US Army also uses ships and other types of water vehicles to move equipment. The navy focuses on ships that are armed and able to fight against threats such as other ships or aircraft. The army uses ships for transportation. Soldiers who serve on army ships have a saying about the roles of the army and the navy and how each uses its ships. They say, "We bring the goods; they bring the guns."

The ships used by the navy and the army are built for different purposes. Each is built to do a specific job or perform a special role. From skimming the surface of the ocean to traveling stealthily beneath its waters, there is a ship for almost everything.

# CHAPTER THREE

# CARRIERS AND BATTLESHIPS

In today's military, more ships than ever are needed to meet specific purposes. More specialized ships are being planned and built every day. Ships are grouped in categories according to their main purpose.

## Prepared to Fight

Battleships were once the fighting ships of the military. They were designed to carry out warfare on

The guided missile cruiser USS San Jacinto patrols the Mediterranean Sea.

The guided-missile destroyer USS Stethem fires a Harpoon missile during an exercise in the Pacific Ocean in 2014.

the ocean. They could also fire missiles and other types of weapons from a safe distance at onshore targets. These ships accompanied other ships such as aircraft carriers, cargo ships, and oil tankers. They protected these ships from enemy threats.

Battleships were very large and heavy. They could weigh as much as 55,000 short tons (50,000 metric tons) and were often more than 800 feet (240 m) long. They had several types of huge guns, some of them up to 70 feet (21 m) long and weighing 120 tons (110 metric tons). These ships were used from the early 1900s until the 1990s. Because they were so large, battleships were vulnerable to smaller, faster ships that could attack and quickly escape them. Torpedoes fired from other ships or submarines could damage or sink them too. The navy no longer uses battleships. Smaller, more specialized ships have taken their place.

Cruisers are lighter fighting ships used mostly in battle. They carry guided missiles and can move swiftly

## Remember the *Maine*

The USS *Maine* is one of the most famous US battleships in history. It exploded in the harbor at Havana, Cuba, in 1898. Most of the crew died, and the ship sank. The cause of the explosion was unknown, but many Americans blamed it on Spain, which controlled Cuba and had forces in the area. The sinking of the *Maine* led to the Spanish-American War later that year. "Remember the *Maine*" became a rallying cry for US troops and supporters of the war.

### Cruisers

**Ticonderoga Class**
Length: 567 feet (173 m)
Displacement: Up to 10,750 short tons
           (9,750 metric tons)
Speed: 30 knots (35 miles per hour)
           (56 km/h)
Crew: 364

### Frigates

**Oliver Hazard-Perry Class**
Length: 445 feet (134 m)
Displacement: Up to 4,600 short tons
           (4,100 metric tons) full load
Speed: 29 knots (33 miles per hour)
           (54 km/h)
Crew: 215

### Destroyers

**Arleigh-Burke Class**
Length: 505 feet (155 m)
Displacement: Up to 10,635 short tons
           (9,500 metric tons) full load
Speed: 30 knots (35 miles per hour)
           (56 km/h)
Crew: 276

## Sizes of Ships

The US Navy uses ships of many different sizes. Compare the three ships shown in the graphic above. Which ship is the longest? Which is the lightest? Which requires the most crew? What types of jobs do you think would be best for each ship?

during battles. They are powered by diesel engines. Cruisers are smaller than battleships. They weigh approximately 10,000 short tons (9,000 metric tons) and are around 600 feet (180 m) long.

Destroyers serve more purposes than cruisers. They carry guided missiles, but they also can be used to support groups of soldiers on aircraft carriers or on land. Like cruisers, they are powered by diesel engines rather than nuclear power.

Frigates are the transportation ships of the military. These ships carry soldiers to their missions. Because they often escort other ships, they carry some weapons for defense. They can also transport supplies.

## Carrier Groups

Aircraft carriers were not only useful as portable landing strips for airplanes. They could also carry heavier weapons. Some old carriers were powered by diesel engines, but the newer ones are powered by nuclear energy. Nuclear fuel is more efficient for ships because a small amount of fuel provides an enormous amount of energy. Nuclear ships can function for several years without refueling.

The USS *George Washington* is a massive Nimitz-class aircraft carrier.

Because a carrier sails in international waters, it provides a place for military airplanes to land without having to get permission from a foreign country. US Navy carriers are actually official US territory. A carrier is so big that it has its own zip code, hospital, barbershop, dental clinic, and gym. Carriers of the Nimitz class are so long that if one was stood on end, it would be almost as tall as the Empire State Building.

There can be between 5,000 and 6,000 people living and working on just one carrier.

These massive ships can store aircraft in hangars below their decks. They also have weapons such as guided missiles, which can be fired at targets in the air or on land. New classes of carriers continue to be developed.

## Gerald R. Ford Class Aircraft Carriers

The newest class of aircraft carriers is the Gerald R. Ford class. They are named for the former US president. Ford-class carriers have new design features and technologies that require less maintenance. Their electrical utilities need less maintenance than those powered by steam. These ships need approximately 700 fewer sailors than does a traditional carrier. The Ford class of carriers were also the first to be designed using 3D computer modeling.

# CHAPTER FOUR

# HOW DID THEY BUILD THAT?

The US Navy has approximately 285 active ships. The number of new ships added every year varies. Building a ship takes a lot of people and raw materials. And it can take years from the time a ship is designed to when it actually touches the water for the first time.

The lower bow unit for the carrier *Gerald R. Ford* is lifted into place. Aircraft carriers are put together one module at a time.

## Piece by Piece

Ships used to be built from the bottom up. This means that the bottom of the ship was built first. Then all the other structures and levels were built inside the hull, or the outer skin of the ship. This also meant that all the construction had to be done in the same place. But new construction methods made it faster and easier to build new ships.

### 3D Modeling

Ships can now be designed using 3D modeling. A full-size model of the entire ship is created using computer graphics. Designers can actually walk around inside the model. All of the ship's systems are included. This process ensures that the ship has all the features it needs. It also makes sure that the ship's equipment and crew will fit in the space and function properly.

Workers build an aircraft carrier as a series of pieces or modules called superlifts. These are sections of the carrier that can include many rooms. They may also include several different stories, or decks. All the

The aircraft carrier *Gerald R. Ford* under construction at Newport News Shipbuilding in Virginia

wiring and plumbing has been connected before the sections are put together. These superlifts can weigh 80 to 900 short tons (73 to 816 metric tons). Most carriers are built using approximately 200 superlifts. Each module is built separately. Then a huge crane lifts each module into its spot inside the growing ship. The module is then welded to the rest of the ship.

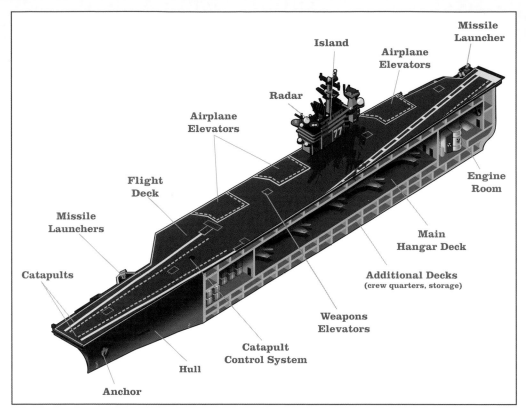

Island

Missile
Launcher

Airplane
Elevators

Radar

Airplane
Elevators

Engine
Room

Flight
Deck

Missile
Launchers

Main
Hangar Deck

Catapults

Additional Decks
(crew quarters, storage)

Weapons
Elevators

Catapult
Control System

Hull

Anchor

## Aircraft Carriers

Aircraft carriers are made up of approximately 1 billion individual parts. These ships have systems for launching airplanes, moving through the water, and taking care of all the people on board. They are divided into specific areas for these systems.

The last module to be installed is called the island. It is the tower command center that sticks up from the flight deck. The island can weigh up to 575 short tons (522 metric tons). Then the ship's four screw propellers, made of bronze, are attached to

An AV-8B Harrier lands on the amphibious assault ship USS *Kearsarge* during sea trials in August 2014.

the ship. A tube connects them to the nuclear reactor turbine that will power the ship. The carrier also has two huge anchors. Each one weighs 30 short tons (27 metric tons), and each link in the chains that are attached to the anchors weighs 360 pounds (163 kg).

Other military ships, such as cruisers and destroyers, are built piece by piece too. Building ships this way is faster because it allows many people to work on the ship at the same time but in different areas.

## Trial and Error

Building a ship is hardly a foolproof process. In 2007 the US Navy conducted sea trials on a new type of ship, an amphibious ship called the USS *San Antonio*. Unfortunately one of its two steering systems failed. The navy also discovered that the ship had major defects in three of the 17 categories it tested. The ship required millions of dollars more to fix the problems. It ended up costing $8 million more than originally budgeted. When the *San Antonio* was finally accepted by the navy and deployed, it developed oil leaks and had to be docked for repairs.

## Taking It for a Spin

Once a ship has been completed, it goes through sea trials. A sea trial is the first time the ship actually sails on the water. Sea trials usually take place out on the open ocean. They can last for a few hours or for several days. All systems are tested and checked to make sure that the ship is safe and reliable. The crew also has its first chance to get a sense for how the new ship feels and steers.

After the sea trials are done, any repairs or changes that are needed will be made.

In 1921 officials from the United States, the United Kingdom, Japan, France, and Italy signed a treaty that limited the number of new warships each nation could build. The countries wanted to prevent one country from trying to become more powerful than the others. Part of the treaty said:

> *The Contracting Powers agree to limit their respective naval armament as provided in the present Treaty. The Contracting Powers may retain respectively the . . . ships which are specified in Chapter II, Part 1. On the coming into force of the present Treaty, but subject to the following provisions of this Article, all other capital ships, built or building, of the United States, the British Empire and Japan shall be disposed of . . . [T]he United States may complete and retain two ships of the West Virginia class now under construction. On the completion of these two ships, the North Dakota and Delaware, shall be disposed of.*

Source: *"Conference on the Limitation of Armament." ibiblio.org. University of North Carolina at Chapel Hill, n.d. Web. Accessed September 23, 2014.*

## Changing Minds

Many ships were scrapped and destroyed as a result of this treaty. Imagine that you are a shipbuilder who is now out of work because of the treaty, and write a letter to your congressperson giving your opinion of the treaty and its results.

# CHAPTER FIVE

# THE NEWEST NAVY SHIPS

Keeping up with modern battle technology means that military ships must constantly be improved. The military is also starting to design ships that can do more than fight or carry aircraft. Some future ships will start out as large empty shells that can be customized to perform specialized duties. This would make it cheaper to build ships for specific purposes.

The joint high speed vessel USNS *Fall River* is one of the newest and most versatile ships used by the US military.

The M80 *Stiletto* is a new ship the navy is testing to patrol shallow waters.

## The Pickup Truck of the Sea

One of the newest military ships is the joint high speed vessel (JHSV). The first JHSV is the USNS *Spearhead*. It is referred to as the "pickup truck of the sea" because it can be used for so many different things. The JHSV is simply a large aluminum shell around four diesel engines. It has two hulls side by side, and a large flight deck sits on top. The navy can take this basic shell and then add special modules or weapons, depending on what is needed. The JHSV is very fast and is not meant for combat. Instead it can move quickly and carry supplies and soldiers. It can also be used to carry medical equipment or work as a staging area for secret missions onshore.

## A Secret Destroyer

The navy also has a new kind of destroyer that is built to be stealthy. The first of these destroyers is the USS *Zumwalt*. It is 610 feet (190 m) long and 80 feet (24 m) wide. That makes it bigger than any other destroyer. But the ship is built with unusual angles that make it much harder to see on radar than a regular ship. On radar, the *Zumwalt* doesn't look any different from a fishing boat.

### M80 *Stiletto*

The navy is working on a new ship to use for patrolling shallow waters. It is called the M80 *Stiletto*. It is made from carbon fiber materials. Its hull is shaped like two side-by-side letter Ms. It can go almost 70 miles per hour (110 km/h), which is very fast for a ship. It captures energy from waves and creates an air cushion for the ship to ride on. This means that it needs less fuel to operate.

## 3D Printing at Sea

In July 2014 the US Navy put a 3D printer on board the USS *Essex*, an amphibious assault ship. It wanted to test how well a 3D printer would work amid the motion of a ship at sea. The printer was used to make gaskets, wrenches, electrical boxes, medical instruments, model airplanes, and specialized tools. The navy hopes that it can also be used make temporary parts for ships until replacement parts arrive from land.

The *Zumwalt* also has a new laser weapon system that can fire at aircraft and small surface ships. The laser system is controlled by one sailor using a console that looks like a video-game controller. Each laser shot is much cheaper than existing weapons and ammunition.

The navy also hopes that someday the *Zumwalt* and other ships will no longer need to be refueled. Instead, they may be able to make their own fuel by taking hydrogen and carbon monoxide out of seawater. This would be cheaper and better for the environment. It would also mean that enemies couldn't destroy the navy's source of fuel as a way to defeat its ships in battle.

Ships are among the most important vehicles that the military uses every day. From fighting to rescue missions to disaster aid, they are vital. And because they are needed and used every day, the military will keep improving them with new technologies. Ships have come a long way since the days of wooden sailing ships. And they will become even more powerful and efficient in the future.

## EXPLORE ONLINE

Chapter Five talks about some of the navy's newest ships, including the USS *Zumwalt*. The website below discusses ways in which the *Zumwalt* might not be a good ship for the navy. As you know, every source is different. How is the information given in the website different from the information in this chapter? What information is the same? How do the two sources present information differently? What can you learn from this website?

**USS** *Zumwalt*
www.mycorelibrary.com/ships

*Allied forces take control of the beach in Normandy, France, during the D-day invasion of 1944.*

## D-day, World War II

D-day was one of the most successful battles of World War II. On June 6, 1944, Allied forces (including soldiers from the United States and the United Kingdom) successfully landed 175,000 troops on five beaches along the coast of France. They were fighting against the German forces that occupied the area. The Allies used many kinds of ships to move troops across the English Channel from Great Britain and onto the beaches. Despite suffering many casualties, the Allies were able to control the beaches. The attack would be the beginning of the end of World War II in Europe.

*The USNS* Comfort *played an important role in helping Haiti recover from a devastating earthquake in 2010.*

## USNS *Comfort*

On January 12, 2010, a massive earthquake struck the country of Haiti. Eight days later, the US Navy hospital ship USNS Comfort anchored off the coast of Haiti and began treating injured and sick earthquake victims. Over the next seven weeks medical personnel on the Comfort performed 843 surgeries, delivered nine babies, and used 10 operating rooms to treat patients. At the height of its mission, the ship received one new patient every six to nine minutes. The Comfort's ability to travel to Haiti quickly helped save many lives at a time when medical facilities in Haiti had been damaged or destroyed by the earthquake.

# STOP AND THINK

## You Are There

This book mentions the role that the USS *Bataan* played in helping bring relief supplies to Haiti after an earthquake in 2010. Imagine that you are a boy or girl who lived in Haiti at that time. How do you feel when US military ships bring supplies to your town? Are you grateful or a little uneasy because they are soldiers and sailors?

## Say What?

Learning about military ships, past and present, can mean learning new vocabulary. Find five words in this book that you've never heard before. They can be ordinary words or technical terms. Use a dictionary to find out what they mean. Then, in your own words, write down their meanings and use each new word in a sentence.

## Surprise Me

This book talks about US naval history and new technology for future ships. After reading this book, what two or three facts about military ships did you find the most interesting or surprising? Write a few sentences about each fact. What made them surprising or interesting to you?

## Why Do I Care?

The US military uses ships for defense and during conflicts. But that is not their only role. What peacetime uses do these ships have? When have they proved valuable at home and around the world? What other nonmilitary uses do these ships have?

# GLOSSARY

**amphibious**
able to live or travel both on land and in water

**cargo**
the freight carried by a vehicle

**hangar**
a building in which aircraft are kept or repaired

**mine**
an explosive device that can be buried underground or placed underwater

**missile**
a weapon that is launched at a target

**module**
a standard part or unit that is used to build a bigger structure

**nuclear**
using energy that comes from splitting atoms

**propeller**
a device with blades that is driven by an engine and used to power a boat or airplane

**stealthy**
done in a secret, cautious way so as not to be noticed

**torpedo**
a cigar-shaped explosive that moves under its own power and explodes when it hits its target

**trial**
the act or process of testing or trying something

# LEARN MORE

## Books

Green, Philip. *Littoral Combat Ship*. Minneapolis,
MN: Bellwether Media, 2011. Print.

Hamilton, John. *Submarines*. Minneapolis, MN:
Abdo Publishing, 2012. Print.

Jackson, Kay. *Navy Ships in Action*. New York:
Powerkids Press, 2009. Print.

## Websites

To learn more about the US military and its resources,
visit **booklinks.abdopublishing.com**. These links are
routinely monitored and updated to provide the most
current information available.

Visit **www.mycorelibrary.com** for free additional tools
for teachers and students.

# INDEX

# ABOUT THE AUTHOR

Marcia Amidon Lusted has written 95 books and 450 magazine articles for young readers. Her husband served in the US Navy and helped build the aircraft carrier USS *Carl Vinson*, then sailed around the world on it.